Journey of Faith

Children's Storybook

Dr. Derrick L. Randolph Sr.

.

ISBN: 1944166009
ISBN-13: 978-1-944166-00-7

Journey of Faith Ministries
contact@journeyoffaithministries.org
www.journeyoffaithministries.org

DEDICATION

I dedicate this book to my children, Derrick L. Randolph Jr. and Joshua Isaiah Randolph.

ACKNOWLEDGMENTS

Thank you to all who contributed to the Journey of Faith for Children
Character illustrations by Raina Ram
Edited by Ashley WonderInk

The Johnson family is taking a walk together

Each family member is
discussing their
experience with God

Tammy recently accepted the Lord as her savior

"Someone shared the gospel of Jesus Christ with me. I believed it, repented of my sins and received salvation through faith in the death and resurrection of Jesus Christ. I am so glad that God forgave me of my sins."

Dad remembers receiving God's revelation

Dad says, "Tammy, God has always sent messengers to tell us about Him. God uses angels, prophets, preachers, friends, and family. They spend time in the presence of God and then deliver a message for us to turn away from a life of sin and turn toward God."

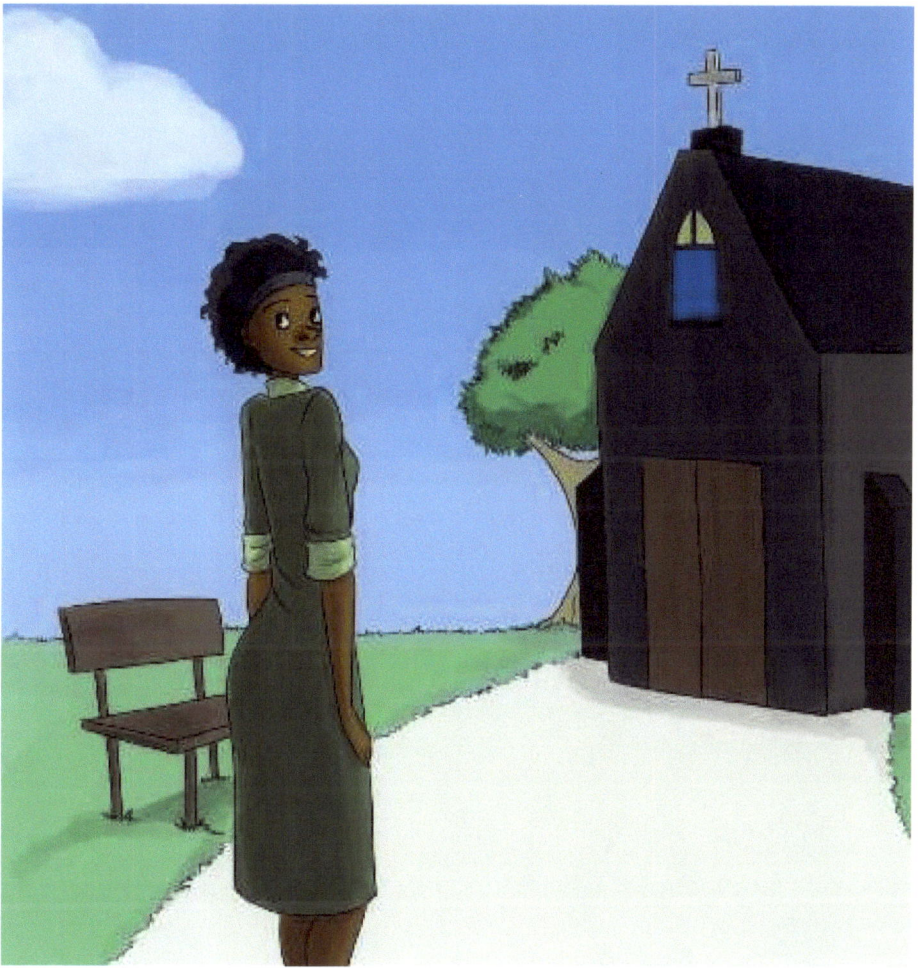

Mom remembers learning about God

"Tammy," Mom says with love. "I remember when I was just learning about God. I could see the beautiful stars in the sky, amazing creatures on the earth, and the power of love in people. Only God could create such beauty. It showed me that God is the creator, and that God has all of the power in the world. There is nothing more special than when you begin to learn about God."

Timothy remembers getting to know God

Timothy says, "Soon you will get to know God for yourself. You will understand how God is the Father, Son and Holy Spirit."

Tammy is becoming a part of Gods church

"My faith in Jesus led me to join the church," Tammy says.
"That's where I connect with other Christians. I enjoy fun and
fellowship with them, When I received baptism and communion
with them through the Lord's Supper, I started a new life as
a member of the church."

Mom tells Tammy about learning the Bible

"Tammy," Mom said. "Soon you will begin to learn the scriptures in the Bible. This is important because God's scriptures are powerful. They help us to become strong and to live in the authority that God gives us."

The family members were on a journey of faith

"Kids," Dad said. "We are on a journey of faith together. We're receiving revelation from God and developing our relationship with God. Look at it like we're going up and down a mountain. Going up is hard. You're learning about God, getting to know God, His church, and His scriptures. Going down the mountain is easier because you're getting stronger, walking in God's grace, receiving deliverance, and developing discipline. As you learn to obey, and even suffer, your life will show God's glory and it is beautiful"

Dad remembers learning to walk in God's grace

"One day," Dad said kindly. "You will begin to learn the *grace* of God, where God walks and talks with you. Here, God starts teaching you His word, His ways, and His promise to be with you. As God has compassion on you, He teaches you to have compassion on others. He will keep teaching you, correcting you, and holding you accountable for what you've learned."

Timothy tells Tammy how hard it was for him

"Mom. Dad," Timothy cuts in. "This journey was not so easy for me.
I kept getting into trouble. It was difficult in many ways, but God
kept rescuing me. See, there's so much more than receiving
eternal salvation. We also receive deliverance and freedom from
all kinds of difficulties and struggles each day. God even rescues
us from all kids of suffering and danger for others' sake so they
will see and believe in God. Then He restores us after we've been
battered by the storms of life."

Mom developed spiritual discipline

"Timothy," Mom said. "Learning to walk with God will become easier. It did for me. I kept getting stronger and stronger because I developed discipline. God taught me to develop the disciplines of the faith, like fasting, prayer, praise, worship, service, and fellowship. They all became a part of my daily and weekly routines. Soon, they helped me become a productive Christian in the kingdom of God."

It got easier for Dad when he learned to obey God

"Timothy," Dad said. "It didn't get easier for me until I learned how to respond to life's challenges. It took loving obedience to God. You may even experience a tougher kind of love. This kind of love demands obedience to God. Only then will you graduate to a fuller measure of faith. Remember, Timothy, your relationship with God is built on love and obedience."

Timothy still suffered affliction from others

"Well," Timothy said sadly. "It never got easy for me. I am still having a hard time in Christ because life is hard and other people harass me. It's like they are against me because I believe in Jesus Christ. It seems like the more I want to live right for God, the more bad things happen."

Mom told Timothy and Tammy it will all be fine

"Listen, Timothy," Mom warned with gentleness. "Just keep walking with the Lord and living a life that gives God all of the glory. It will all work out just fine. Your suffering will help you become mature in Christ. When your relationship with God is attacked, your life will appear to fall apart, but trust me, you will always bounce back. This process is pleasing to God because the Holy Spirit that was in Jesus Christ is being formed in you too. Now, I can talk about it because I have been through it. Daughter, look forward to your journey. It is the journey of your faith. It all works to reveal the glory of God."

The End

Journey of Faith
Children's Storybook

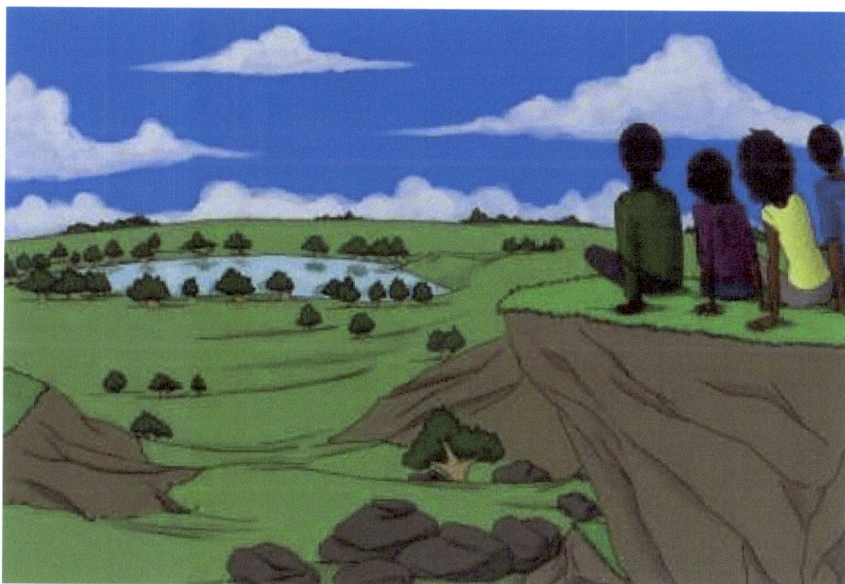

Journey of Faith Ministries

ABOUT THE AUTHOR

Dr. Derrick L Randolph, Sr. is from Baltimore, Maryland.